To Lee & Kryon
& Monica

DNA WAKE UP

A Simple Guide to DNA Activation

With Much Love
& Appreciation

Elizabeth J. Clark

Liz & Lynne

lizfriendly@yahoo.com

To Lynne Atkins
a constant ally in all my adventures.

*

CONTENTS

*

A huge Thank You to
Lee Carroll and Kryon
for exposing us all to the wonders of our Divinity
within the Twelve Layers of our DNA.

*

With great appreciation to my dearest friend
Patrice Thomas
for her unconditional love and constant support.

*

And, of course, gratitude to my mother
Patricia I. Clark
for sharing her DNA and positive outlook.

*

FOREWORD

We are all spiritual beings incarnate upon this earthly, three dimensional, linear plane. Within our bodies divinity lies waiting for our call. We long for this connection, not knowing it has always been within us and is awaiting our acknowledgement. As you begin this study of Metaphysical DNA, take time daily to communicate internally using your innate wisdom, allowing your DNA to activate you. This divine power within you is nothing short of miraculous! Tap into your God-self and feel nurtured by the universe, for you are a child of God! You will notice a difference within yourself and you will begin to understand that we are all much more than mere flesh and blood. Open yourself up to all that you are, for your

DNA stands ready to assist in your personal self-discovery.

DNA:

DeoxyriboNucleic Acid (Dee-ahk-see-rye-boh-New-clay-ik Acid).

Your DNA tells an amazing story—the story of Life itself. For the past four billion years or so, since the beginning of time, DNA has been the chemical of life. Everything that has ever lived, or now lives, on the planet has DNA, just as you do. Your DNA is the 'map' specific to you and only you! It's what created you in the very first place and it's what defines and identifies you as a unique individual. Your DNA is in every one of your cells from the hair on your head to the tip of your toes, and it is working every day, hour, minute, and second, creating the 'you' that is your physical body! Now you might think this all sounds pretty 'scientific' but this is NOT a science book. This is a book about possibility.

It's no secret that the majority of scientific studies support the idea that, on a biological and quantum level, our DNA is the key to our 'make up.' Yet, science can only account for the function of a small amount—about 3%—of our DNA, so for many years the other 97% was considered functionless junk left over from the evolutionary process. That view has been seriously questioned of late, especially after completion of the Human Genome Project in 2003. Fewer and fewer people are accepting this explanation of 'Junk DNA'. What could be happening in this huge amount of genetic material that no one can explain? NOTHING? Can we honestly believe it's just 'excess baggage'? No way, something is going on within us that we are just beginning to discover. There is something incredibly powerful in that 97%, something that we can connect to and affect within us. It is the energy of our spirituality, where our 'divinity' resides, with the ability to activate our physical body and our higher self. We can communicate innately with that part of us! We can wake up our makeup and guide our DNA as simply as putting our attention to it.

It is time to understand this inner truth, the truth of Human DNA and its mysterious abilities. All you need to do is tune in, communicate and allow your DNA to do what it was designed by The Creator to do. The key is to awaken yourself to your Metaphysical DNA, the doing of which could change EVERYTHING in your physical life. For the piece of God that lives in you is lying in wait, listening for your pure intentions to begin its activation of all that you are.

*

SCIENCE AND DNA

DNA: (Deoxyribonucleic Acid) A nucleic acid that contains a genetic code of instructions used in the development and functioning of all known living organisms.

We have all heard about DNA. We studied required information about organisms, cells and molecules while in school. Most people can still remember the basics. However, once school was out, the need to know the specifics of DNA was no longer necessary. Hearing modern science discuss and report on genetic engineering, cloning, genetic disorders and genetic predispositions has brought DNA back into the spotlight. These discussions, however fascinating, continued to keep DNA in the realm of exciting, yet mystifying, information to the lay person. However important DNA and its use is, it still belonged to scientists and medical professionals.

In 1990 The Human Genome Project set out to map and identify the sequence of chemical base pairs which make up DNA, approximately 20,000–25,000 genes of the human genome. During these studies it was determined that 97% of the human genome does not encode protein sequences. That 97%—or 'Junk DNA'—has no known function.

The term 'Junk DNA' carries with it implications which you would not expect 'Junk DNA', or the new discoveries that have been made in this area, to elicit. It has become apparent that the phrase 'Junk DNA' hits some very core belief systems of many scientists. Discussions of this topic have created some very large and passionately heated debates concerning the implications these discoveries have upon theories of creation, Darwinism vs. Intelligent Design fueled by 'Junk DNA'. Could you have imagined that the controversy of 'Junk DNA' relates directly to one's personal belief in God? As we look closer you will see why this is so.

Darwinian Evolution is described as a four billion year old process, creating life forms, primarily at random, but each shaped by an ever changing and complex environment that has resulted in all the wondrous life around us. Darwinists argue that 'Junk' DNA, or non-protein-coding portions of DNA, are remnants from the evolutionary process, no longer needed for survival.

Intelligent Design has been described as the proposition that certain features of the Universe and of living things are best explained by an intelligent cause. Intelligent Design proponents claim there is a purpose for this 97%, it is not junk, we have simply not discovered its purpose yet.

According to Jonathan Wells in 'The Myth of Junk DNA',

"Our genome is increasingly revealing itself to be a multidimensional, integrated system in which non-protein-coding DNA is performing a wide variety of functions… Even apart from possible implications for Intelligent Design, however, the demise of the myth of junk DNA promises to stimulate scientists willing to follow the evidence wherever it leads."

Each individual innately knows that something 'more' exists. Could this something more be found within the 97% of our 'Junk' DNA? Life is a miracle from all angles, a magical wonder. You can feel the excitement and celebration of such a marvel in the existence of 'All That Is'. Try to feel the truth within yourself, with your own instinctive knowing. Could this 'Junk DNA' be the part of God within you? We all possess the intelligence to create, an intuitive intelligence that lies within us, within our DNA. In this we are truly co-creators. As you delve into the metaphysical aspects of your DNA, I put forward the theory that this 'Junk DNA' is indeed where your divinity lies and use of this 97%—through consciously aware conversation—is the key to your individual discovery of God, your higher self and your spiritual evolution.

*

It's true we are much more than flesh and blood. We have DNA and within this lies the universe!

Yes, within you is a space so tiny it is as big as forever.

Seems strange?

Transcendental is our lot. The small goes on forever as does the large. In the cosmos and the microscopic an 'end' cannot be found.

Why is this? Because infinity loops around.

Growing, becoming, enlarging and shrinking. This is a world in motion, an eternity that is alive.

How can we wrap our minds around such vibrant concepts?

Feel it and you will 'know'. Sense the fluid movement.

Our DNA never rests, it is always renewing, recreating itself and becoming more. Science can find all this but it is your knowing that makes it real.

Within this process is a secret that can no longer be kept still. Divinity lies within! See yourself as the source. Celebrate God within, become all that you are.

It is inevitable for we are evolving and our true nature will be revealed. Oneness will be known.

TWELVE LAYERS OF
SPIRITUAL DISCOVERY

What is essential to spiritual growth is conscious awareness; for once a truth has been found it will never be lost! You cannot 'not know' a thing that has been made known to you. Once you learn about recycling plastic, and the importance of this to the environment, it becomes impossible to discard a plastic drink bottle in good conscience without trying to find a recycle bin for it. This same principle is also true when working with DNA. Learning the basic spiritual concepts of your DNA opens a floodgate of knowing and healing as well as individual spiritual evolution. More than chemistry, ringing of truth and a higher power, your DNA has a story to tell. This story is filled with the love of God and a sacred life powered by the joy of creation.

Human DNA is where God and man meet in the mix of physical and metaphysical, vibrating with the truth of who you are, 'a piece of God' in physical form. Within the sacred double helix at the atomic level there is a master plan, your awareness of this truth will open your eyes and send you on a mystical journey towards expanded human consciousness. Your DNA is perfect and need not be improved, it does not need to be activated but is ready, lying in wait for your instructions to activate your physical body as well as your higher consciousness! You will initiate this activation by delving into a deeper understanding of each of the twelve layers. So, let's begin your discovery of who you truly are through the portal provided by your DNA, connecting to Spirit itself! This will be a personal journey as no two humans have the exact same DNA. Your individual DNA creates the informational instructions that keep your body going and your connection with Spirit strong. Within this same DNA also exist twelve layers lying in wait for your 'wake up', directed by your specific attention and intent.

Open your mind with an intention to understand these twelve layers of DNA from an etheric perspective to expand your individual awareness. It is important to understand these layers are enmeshed and interact with one another, although defined separately they are not separate from each other. Interdimensionally, consider your DNA as a vortex or a portal to a much larger understanding. The vibration of these truths can be found by venturing consciously through the twelve layers, allowing them to activate YOU!

*

GROUP ONE:
LAYERS ONE, TWO AND THREE

GROUP ONE consists of the first three layers creating a foundation which is grounded in the third dimension, the physical. These first three layers act as the platform from which the physical body arises calling out to the divine; the framework of our holistic being. It is from here we begin our understanding of all the potentials which exist within each Human Being.

Layer ONE: This layer resides in the third dimensional world yet is multidimensional in its communication with all other layers. Acting as a conduit layer one connects the physical to the metaphysical. It serves as the messenger, for layer one is at one with all others and is the core. Seen as the double helix, layer one represents your chemistry as well as your multidimensional parts, a bridge receiving and transmitting, taking information from the other layers and implementing it upon your gene structure. Grounded and attached to the physical, layer one is your blueprint, serving as the biological instructions for this lifetime with the ability to alter your physical being, by utilizing the influences of all other layers.

As you connect with layer one, by activating your intent, it will become aware of your conscious thought, giving instructions to your protein-encoded protons and expanding your spiritual being in alignment with higher consciousness.

Layer TWO: Calling out with the questions, 'Who am I?', 'Why am I here?' and 'What should I do?' layer two is a personal layer. There is a characteristic of duality here, two concepts within a singular consciousness, the flesh and blood, biological Human Being who also is a piece of God with free choice. This layer is responsible for providing a sense of purpose and meaning within each of us. Something calls to you from this layer, a knowing of direction and a feeling of significance. An unexplainable quest, calling you to become more than mere flesh and blood, moving you beyond your temporal self, expanding into all of the universe.

As you connect with layer two, by activating your intent,

you will become aware of your lessons or missions being brought forward from the spiritual to the physical.

Layer THREE: An action layer, layer three is the master within you, directing the chemistry in your body to become what your consciousness calls for. It increases the power of your cellular structure with your increased awareness, adjusting the vibration of the whole DNA molecule. Childlike and filled with joy, listening for changes in consciousness, layer three never changes but is what changes the other layers and the chemistry of the body to assist with spiritual AWAKENING! Layer three delivers the 'Ah-ha' or 'God knowing' moments within us all that moves the simple Human Being from a meaningless physical existence into a wider spiritually awakened state.

As you connect with layer three, by activating your intent, you will become aware of an increased energy, enabling you to rise above your physical being and clearly see your path to spiritual expansion.

*

These first three layers of DNA can be seen as an image of a beautiful budding and blossoming flower. The stem, layer one, rooted to the physical, connecting all; the bud, layer two, filled with possibility of purpose; and the blossom, layer three, opened to the expanse of creation. This flower is grounded, connected and reaching for the sun, in the same way we reach for our divine source.

Group ONE

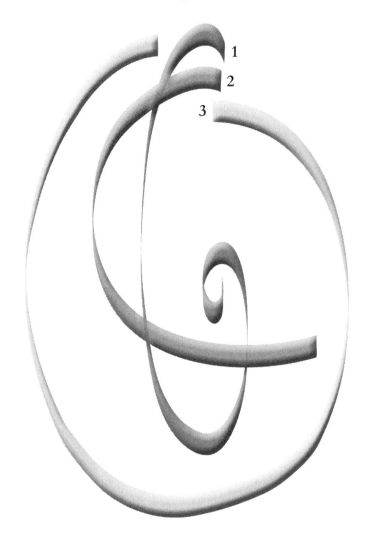

Layers One, Two and Three

GROUP ONE EXERCISES

Layer ONE

Focusing on this biological layer, feel your strength and power over yourself.

How will you direct that?

What message will you send to the rest of your DNA?

Contact has been made; what does that feel like?

Layer TWO

Feel your vitality and worth, dissolve duality and see yourself as perfect!

If you have any issues within yourself that do not please you, can you see a virtue in them?

Feel the support of layer one and the presence of all other layers strong within you. Do you feel confident?

How does this power feel?

Layer THREE

You are the director of the orchestra that is your DNA, what kind of song do you hear?

Feel your spirit entwined with your body, how do you feel this connection manifesting through layer one?

Feel your personal strength and wisdom through layer two, allow your foundation to be strong!

Call upon layer three to 'awaken and activate' your DNA.

Are you poised to step into 'All That You Are'? What emotions does this understanding bring forward in you?

GROUP ONE

The first three layers create a foundation which is grounded in the third dimension.

Envision yourself standing on a foundation made of these three layers, not as layers but as energies.

What does it look like?

How does it feel?

Do you feel or see any colors or sounds? Describe them.

Alive, vibrant and connected, name some additional feelings you are having in your new awareness.

*

NOTES

You have an armor of love and light,
it wards off any fear.
For what's to fear since you're divine
and death does not come near.

The little spark inside of you,
in every single cell.
Your DNA is empowering,
there's no way that you can fail.

Projecting out from these little sparks,
emitting love and light.
Protecting you from your own self
and demons of the night.

No lurky, scary, darky things can penetrate your love.
Even when projected by your own misguided shrugs.

The light so bright you see your drama
and let your issues go.
So quickly now with your armor strong,
you can feel your power grow.

Allow the oneness of humankind to set your worries free.
Now you create with love and light, so let all others be.

With appreciation and compassion from within,
fears become a mist whose effects are dim.

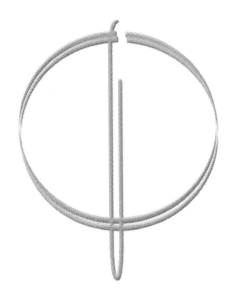

GROUP TWO:
LAYERS FOUR, FIVE AND SIX

We have now begun to discover the meaning and wisdom that lies within the Human DNA on a quantum level. Remember that these layers all work with each other; interacting, overlapping and melding as one. We will continue to divide the metaphysical layers into sections for a better understanding within our linear world. Keep this in mind as you set forth on the second part of our journey—group two, layers four, five and six.

GROUP TWO, consisting of layers four, five and six, is a melding of the human and the divine, which call out your name with a sound and vibration unique to each individual. More metaphysical and less physical than group one, group two becomes less clearly definable. These layers express 'you' as, not only an individual, but also as part of the divine presence of all that is. It is your angelic fingerprint, so to speak. The song of your soul singing in celebration of YOU!

Layers FOUR and FIVE: These two layers act as one, together creating and expressing your true self. They are your angelic name or your God-family name. So strong is your vibration and your song that they cannot be contained in one layer! Not existing in full form, the spiritual soul has been divided and altered to allow us to be here on earth. These two layers intertwine, connecting each human being to themselves, each other and your individual guides and angels. A linking which comes from God and resides within you. These two layers connect and name not only your presence here on earth, but the part of you left behind yet still joined beyond the veil. Expressing the essence of your divinity in this lifetime here on earth, layers four and five always dance together.

As you connect with layers four and five, by activating your intent, your complete essence merges the duality of this earthly and heavenly plane, personalizing your place within it during this lifetime. These layers express your individual existence and create a record of you.

Layer SIX: The God in you! This layer calls out the name of your higher self, vibrating higher than your physical human cellular structure. Filled with the essence of love, it is the channel connecting you to God and is always available in your DNA. A layer filled with comfort and excitement. Layer six is also known as the golden thread. As you learn to love yourself your ability to interface with God creates a pathway to manifestation in your DNA. When you realize the divinity within you, things will begin to change in your life. This is the layer associated with your ability to talk to God, your union to heaven! So you see, YOU are not just a single little self, wandering on the earth, but a representation of a much larger all-encompassing presence of God. A representation of all that is, incarnate upon this planet, always sitting in communication with God.

As you connect with layer six, by activating your intent, you become in tune with God and open a direct line of communication with the divine. This union has always been within you and, with your expanded awareness, God's presence will become more evident.

*

Group TWO

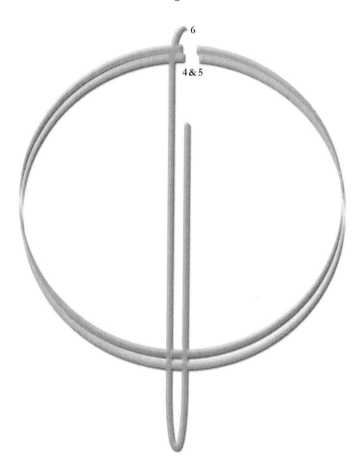

Layers Four, Five and Six

GROUP TWO EXERCISES

Layers FOUR and FIVE

Focusing on layers four and five, quiet your mind and listen.

Feel your individual vibration existing around and through you, describe what you feel.

Do you recognize your name in the feeling and sound?

While in this space begin to hum, bringing together the many parts of you.

What does your song sound like?

Layer SIX

Allow yourself to feel the love of God coming into you. How does it feel to be loved so unconditionally?

Is there anything that would prevent you from feeling this way towards yourself?

Acknowledge that this unconditional love, this vibration, is also coming from YOU! Merge these energies and feel the oneness of God within, while releasing any doubt of your worthiness to be loved unconditionally.

What is the prayer you offer to yourself?

GROUP TWO

Layers four, five and six are the melding of the human and the divine, which calls out your multidimensional name.

Expressing the energies of your soul and God's love as one, allow yourself to feel the strength of all that you are.

How clear is your vibration?

Describe the overlap of your God energy and your individual energy within you.

Once enveloped in self-love what will you release?

GROUPS ONE and TWO

You are perfectly incarnate with a strong foundation from your grounding layers one, two and three. See and feel layers four, five and six intertwined with this grounding, establishing your individuality as well as your oneness with all of creation.

Can you describe this?

How does it feel?

What do you sound like?

This is the call of who you truly are on earth, vibrating and expressing your divinity!

NOTES

The Trinity Within Humankind

A human Soul comes into a Body and with it is a connection to Source, and with this we have created a trinity. A sturdy tripod to grow upon. Each of us is supported from within and around and about. We give little notice to our physical growth, it goes on without attention. We feel the Soul and recognize sudden changes occurring there. Euphoric step by euphoric step, a Master begins to emerge. Attention is given to Soul and Source but what of your physical vibration?

Align all three—the All of You—and wake up your physical presence, for within you lives the wholeness.

Hidden within your DNA a magical truth lies dormant. As dormant as your Soul before you awakened it. As dormant as Source until you called.

The earth is a place of free choice, free will is ripe on this planet. But once you call, all three respond and you're alive inside and out. Touch base with your Body, Soul and Source. Within yourself three dynamics dwell, awaiting your call to come forward.

Talk to your Body so often forgotten, wake up your DNA makeup!

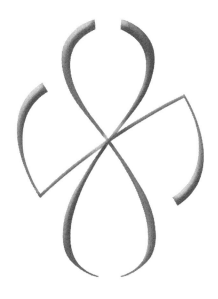

GROUP THREE:
LAYERS SEVEN, EIGHT AND NINE

As you continue on with the discoveries that exist in your twelve Metaphysical Layers of DNA, keep in mind that these teachings are open to your individual interpretation. Feel your way, within your own DNA, to your inner knowing and healing as well as your individual spiritual evolution. Filled with the love of God you become co-creator of your own spiritual path. Your journey towards activation continues with the description of group three, DNA layers seven, eight and nine.

GROUP THREE, made up of layers seven, eight and nine, this group has been touched by Angels!

Humankind has evolved into one basic kind of being without the variations we find in other mammals. Having been seeded by what can be described as Angelic Forces or Divine Intervention, group three represents the core of what differentiates us from other mammals, that which creates our connection and memory of home, the house of God. It is felt as a vibrational calling and drives our longing for home. Within these layers we find a record of human history upon the earth as well as our individual history, which will bring alignment and true healing.

Layer SEVEN: Powering your search for home, beyond the veil towards your union with God, your call towards divinity lies within this layer. The trumpets of heaven can be heard surrounding this layer; they play a familiar melody in a language of love and light. It is the nagging presence drawing you inward to your connection with your source, affirming that we are all one, united by this angelic seed within us. Humankind has been bestowed with the seed of creation! This layer is a gift from God through divine intervention and is a quality that sets us apart from all other mammals. It prompts spiritual awareness, continually sparking the search for the divine presence within you and all humankind.

As you connect with layer seven, by activating your intent, acknowledging the call of an interdimensional reality, which is no longer separated from your earthly reality, the call of God and your way home will become lucid.

Layer EIGHT: This layer, also an angelic gift, is your connection to all the knowledge of your soul's existence upon the earth. Acting as a personal library, layer eight contains the connection to your master record, or the imprint you have left upon the earth. This is an earth based aspect which does not exist without your physical being and is a personal record of YOU, not just your physical being but your soul and its journey here on earth. Within your DNA lies access to a celestial library, celebrating all you have ever been and contain aspects of you which influence this lifetime, creating the largest part of who you are. Accessing your records through layer eight is a powerful tool in your spiritual growth, for it calls on the wisdom and responsibilities of your past.

As you connect with layer eight, by activating your intent, you will be lifted with a remembrance of the journey of your soul upon the earth and your connection to the earth throughout time.

Layer NINE: This layer is very exciting for most people for it is the healing layer, a gift from God presented to us by divine intervention. It calls for your attention to assist in the healing of the physical being. Layer nine is the bridge to ascension, to healing, to self-worth and mastery. Working with layer one, which resides in the third dimensional world yet is also multi-dimensional, you create an action of healing. With its awareness of the synchronization of a whole and healthy cell structure, layer nine seeks balance. Awakening the body's ability to heal, through conscious intent, it is often the missing component in medicine and increases the effectiveness of modern day treatments. Through this layer your body 'knows' what is needed to call forth for physical recovery. Designed to create healing through prayer, meditation, worship, faith and positive thinking, miracles occur, for there is nothing stronger than human intent!

As you connect with layer nine, by activating your intent, 'expect miracles'. Allow yourself to be influenced by your own innate wisdom acting on this internal guidance, for it comes from God. Your physical body will take action.

*

Group THREE

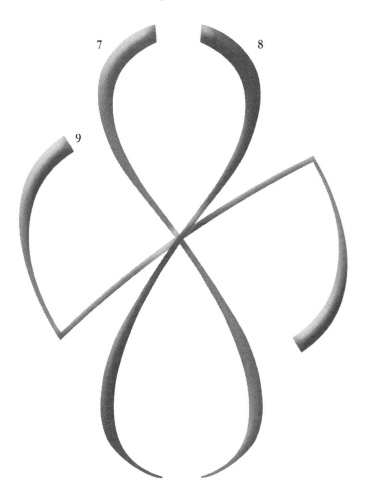

Layers Seven, Eight and Nine

GROUP THREE EXERCISES

Layer SEVEN

When and how did you first begin your search for a creator?

Think about what separates human beings from other mammals.

Divinity lies within you! Do you find comfort in this?

What would you ask of God if you were speaking to yourself?

Layer EIGHT

Give yourself permission to access your personal library.

What skill/wisdom would you like to possess again?

Write a short story or paragraph about an unknown individual who has lived on the earth and had the skills/wisdom you seek.

How does it feel when you read it? Could this have been you?

Layer NINE

Sit still and 'feel' your physical body. Are you aware of imbalance or dis-ease?

How does this feel?

With this awareness ask your cells, your DNA, for guidance toward healing. What might stop you from trusting your personal healing process?

Talk to your DNA daily for four days. Keep a journal and review this on day five. When reviewing your notes can you see a call for action?

GROUP THREE

Elevating us from all other mammals, how do these layers impact your responsibility on Earth?

Feel the strength of the sword/power of God created by these layers within you.

What will you call this sword and how will you keep it sharp?

GROUPS ONE, TWO and THREE

Grounded, Humanly Divine and Angelically Seeded, surround yourself with love. Focus on this new understanding of the first nine layers.

Welcome this new knowledge!

Answer the following questions in one sentence, quickly!

What am I?

Who am I?

How am I?

Elizabeth J. Clark

NOTES

GROUP FOUR:
LAYERS TEN, ELEVEN AND TWELVE

You have now explored the first three groups of your
Metaphysical DNA, layers one through nine. As your
knowledge builds, so should your excitement! You are on
the cusp of living your full potential, becoming the
creator you were divinely designed to be. Allow yourself
to accept your power and connection to God. Within this
three dimensional life, your Metaphysical DNA carries
your divinity. You are a magnificent human being! Allow
the innate wisdom of your DNA to activate you! The
fourth and final grouping of your DNA contains the seat
of God.

GROUP FOUR consists of the final three layers of our Metaphysical DNA. Representing the seat of God within, these layers exist simply in a state of 'being', acting as the structure for everything, the God in us! In contrast to group one, these layers do not exist in the physical at all but, rather, are celestial and are the eternal framework of our being. Existing everywhere, the layers of group four cannot be segmented for they are the essence of all that is. God in a pure sense.

Layer TEN: Fully etheric, this layer speaks of celestial faith and is an essence which touches all other layers. Igniting your very existence, you will know this layer as it calls to you in the synchronicities of your evolving spirituality. Layer ten is a fully active energy in every Ascended Master who has lived upon this earth. Expressing as a spark within, it opens you to the wonderful possibility of believing in God, the glint through the door that calls you inward towards God. Powered by free choice and human intent, this layer gives life meaning and sits, waiting to be summoned. Once you hear the call and allow the feeling, your life will change forever, for it is the foundation of faith, assisting you in discovering your spirituality on your own, with grace and understanding.

As you connect with layer ten, by activating your intent, your true journey begins, all possibilities become limitless, aided by the power and presence of God.

Layer ELEVEN: This layer is vibrating with pure compassion and a gentle energy which brings a balance to humankind's aggressive evolutionary instincts to survive. As with all the layers in this group, standing, waiting to be called upon, layer eleven brings together the best of both male and female aspects. This can be seen in the world's Ascended Masters who radiate strength, compassion and balance. Encompassing the compassion of God, which is the most powerful force in the Universe, this layer, once called on, will soften the hearts of humanity and bring about peace not only individually, but will turn the world towards love and understanding. Calm yet powerful, it sings out with the gentle hum of God's breath.

As you connect with layer eleven, by activating your intent, you will bring harmony to duality, compassionately allowing a transition to balance, becoming a peaceful human being, one with God.

Layer TWELVE: With God being known as the pure, transcendent energy of existence beyond physical form or definition, layer twelve represents God! Your Creator, the celestial force of life and the energy of all that is, serves as your framework. This layer is the fundamental nature of God, which is within you, vibrating at the highest level, eternally, in, through and as everything! It is the pure unconditional love of God that exists everywhere and is within all things existing on both sides of the veil, physical and metaphysical. Sparking your own intuition, this layer is the life force of God, within every person upon the planet. Blending together with the physical, God—as a transcendent energy—is in everything in existence including YOU, the Divine Human Being!

As you connect with layer twelve, by activating your intent, you take the hand of God, the energy of the cosmos and become intuitively inspired, allowing yourself to be all that you truly are, a piece of God!

*

Group FOUR

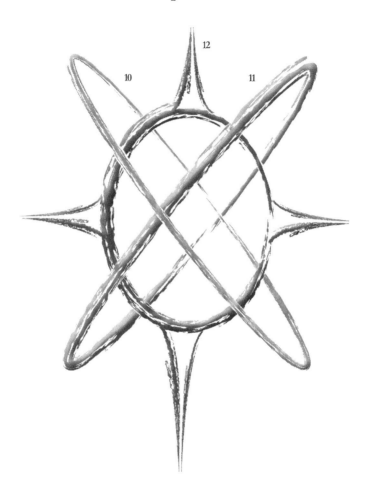

Layers Ten, Eleven and Twelve

GROUP FOUR EXERCISES

Layer TEN

How would you describe your intuition?

You have had 'synchronicities' in your life, give three examples.

Does anything prevent you from knowing this comes from God?

What can you do with any doubts to allow God to flow more easily?

Trust your inner wisdom for it is born of God and lives within you!

Layer ELEVEN

Take a few quite moments to call upon your feminine energy, activating your personal balance with compassion and strength.

Compassion is ripe in this layer, how can you be more compassionate to yourself?

Are there any individuals that call for your understanding?

In what way could you offer them compassion?

Layer TWELVE

Spend a few minutes focusing on your personal vision of God, feel God.

Close your eyes and surround yourself with this powerful, unconditional vibration.

There is nothing more to do here but MELD and feel this as the divine life force within you!

GROUP FOUR

Calling forth the powerful, compassionate God within and without, compose a list of your greatest attributes.

Once this list is complete, quickly describe how these attributes have and can serve you, for in doing so you serve not only yourself, but God and all others.

*

Elizabeth J. Clark

NOTES

The Twelve Metaphysical Layers

Groups ONE through FOUR

A visualization for your activation:

Place your feet firmly on the ground, feeling the power of the earth and your human body combined. Visualize your twelve strands of Metaphysical DNA, millions of times over, throughout your physical body. Know that you are more than other mammals for the seed of God has been planted within you. Embrace the divinity within, while sending out the call (instructions) to activate your higher consciousness.

Now just be calm and listen to your intuition, for you will forevermore know the feeling of your truth and be guided by God!

Be the God that you are, just like everyone else!

*

DNA ACTIVATED

Upon completing your study of The Twelve Metaphysical Layers of DNA, you will not be able to help but feel humbled by the knowledge you have gained. You will have recognized 'God' is all over, around and through all of creation, with us and as one in us and every other human being. Seeded in everything! An all-powerful God energy is awaiting your conscious intent, this knowing will fill you with awe! An awe that will turn into compassion as you realize all other human beings have this in their DNA as well but have not looked to see or feel it. Whether or not it is mentally acknowledged, we are all part God, one and the same! Allow yourself to feel the euphoria and sheer joy of the limitless potential you hold!

WE ALL HOLD! In the acceptance of our Godhood we can all become Masters! The Love of God is everywhere, in everything!

As you continue to focus on the process of discovering and tuning into each of your Twelve Metaphysical Layers of DNA, you will effect an alternate path. This path bridges the physical and the metaphysical, connecting the higher self, spiritual human and the physically incarnated, earthly human in such a way that will inspire the melding of duality upon this earthly plane. No longer will tough choices have to be made, for situations will become clear. Together, the activated human and Mother Earth will create a divinely guided existence, inspired by the enlightened DNA within each of us. God will be found in you and in the oneness of all that we are together. God lives within each of us and, with the knowledge of this, things will never be the same again.

You are one with God and the power within you is
ABSOLUTE!

*

DNA

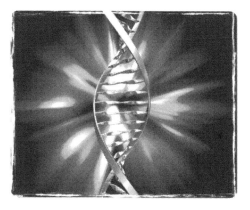

Divine **N**atural **A**lignment

*

Winding, twisting and making more
DNA lives in our core

To magic and wonder, it is the key
For we are so much more than what we see

Talk to yourself and listen too
There is so much more that you can do

A whisper in a quiet place
Discovery in such a tiny space

Where God, our history, our true self sits
Awaiting your call to begin to assist

For you are in charge, you run the show
Wake up your makeup and let yourself grow

*

COMMUNICATING WITH YOUR DNA

Everyone can talk to their individual DNA. It is an innate communication that can be easily achieved. You can start today with some simple practices. As time goes by, your relationship with your Metaphysical DNA will strengthen. Trust in your inner wisdom to guide your continued dialog. You are merely connecting to yourself and to God, the totality of all that you are.

Statements of Empowerment

It has been discovered by Dr. V. Poponin, a renowned quantum physicist, that DNA is susceptible to receiving information from an outside source*, which confirms that DNA indeed responds to outside communication.

With this in mind, begin to talk to your own DNA. Begin simply with statements of acknowledgement and empowerment. Accepting that this communication is innate; start having conversations with your DNA. Say or think things like, "I know that you are building new DNA every second in every bit of me, so build new healthy strands", "Build strands not in old patterns of disease but as whole and new", "You know what you are doing, don't be lazy and just copy old dysfunctional DNA, make new healthy strands 100% PURE."

Know that you are also speaking from your DNA as you make these statements, for the wisdom of your higher self also resides within your DNA, even going so far as reminding your DNA to 'wake you up' to the things that may already be known to you and stimulate your awareness to the synchronicities in your life. You may find yourself rambling on, declaring statement after statement about what you want your DNA to do. This is OK. You are giving instructions to the powerful engine that is creating more DNA every second of every minute of every hour.

*http://www.rexresearch.com/gajarev/gajarev.htm
*http://www.soulsofdistortion.nl/dna2.html

DNA Chanting

Chanting is an ancient practice that has long been used as a way of aligning oneself with spirit. It has been used as an application to bring an individual into a place of focused intent. Begin a routine of morning 'DNA' chanting. You will find it to be a fantastic way to get your day started in a direction of positive expectation for healing and wellbeing. In addition, as you chant, open yourself up to the wisdom housed within your DNA. Tuning into the divine guidance and higher intuition that resides within, open yourself to the realm of limitless possibilities.

There are no rules, in fact finding your own way of attuning yourself can be a very powerful expression! Gone are the days of sitting for hours practicing under the guidance of a guru. Humankind has evolved into beings that are capable of tapping into their own higher selves.

Explore different expressions, rhythms and tones in your chanting! You may simply repeat the letters 'D..N..A' slowly as you exhale through your mouth and again 'D..N..A' as you inhale through your nose, with the knowledge that within your DNA resides your divine connection. With no detailed expectation, but with your focused intent of wellbeing, allow the letters to wrap around themselves, twisting and expanding as they do in the double helix, all the while finding harmony.

Visualization

We all know that DNA cannot be seen with the naked eye. But, did you know that each of your cells has forty-six chromosomes and each chromosome is one long piece of DNA? If you were to stretch out the DNA from those forty-six chromosomes and lay it end to end, it would be over four feet in length. Yet this DNA is coiled up inside the nucleus of a single cell. And you could fit ONE THOUSAND nuclei (new-clee-eye) across the period at the end of this sentence. What is equally amazing is you could fit ONE MILLION threads of DNA across the period at the end of this sentence. Currently, studies are underway indicating that DNA is a loop instead of a strand! WOW! How can we visualize such a seemingly mysterious thing?

*

Many scientific and artistic representations have been created of DNA. Within this book you will find artistic expressions, which I was inspired to create, of the Metaphysical Layers of DNA conveyed in combinations creating the four groups and also the twelve layers as a whole. You will find these images to be very useful for your visualization processes.

Use these images in meditation and expand upon them, surrounding them with beauty and love. Know that this vibrant representation of your DNA is within you a thousand fold, creating and renewing. Play with the feeling, colors and clarity, allowing movement and transformation. As long as you are feeling good, so is your DNA!

*

Breathing Exercise

The average human breathes twenty times a minute, breathing in oxygen in exchange for waste (carbon dioxide), your DNA becoming fresh and rejuvenated with each breath.

To breathe in air and feel the life it brings to you is more magical than you know. Breathing in brings not only life, but the empowerment of all those who have previously exhaled. The spirit of each human soul upon the planet has taken in this same air, after which it is expelled and exchanged/cleaned by nature (Mother Earth, Gaia), never leaving the earth. This air circulates around the world, it is something we all share.

In breathing out we expel all that is unnecessary, releasing what's not needed. This happens naturally, your body sloughs off the useless air that does not harmonize while releasing toxins.

Find calm comfort, listen to your breath. It is ancient air that surrounds the earth, filled with everything you would ever want to know. Fill your lungs with life, wisdom and knowing. Exhale what does not serve you.

Visualize your DNA becoming whole and empowered, feel the creation of newly awakened DNA as you breathe. This vital life force, your breath, is also the breath of God. Your awareness is being activated by newer, younger, healthier DNA.

*

Breathe in and take all that you need.
Breathe out what's left behind.

Health in
Ill out

Wisdom in
Dullness out

Love in
Hate out

Abundance in
Lack out

Strength in
Weakness out

Opportunity lies in your breath; it's something you can't
live without, so you might as well direct it!

*

KINESIOLOGY

Another way of communicating with your DNA is Kinesiology, a practice of asking your body what it wants. You have been created with an innate intelligence and it knows everything about you! Your DNA knows ALL about you and what is going on inside. Tap into this wisdom and discover a system that communicates to you on a personal level.

You can talk to your DNA, to get your body regenerating itself and to tap into your divinity, broadening your understanding of yourself, the world and even the universe. Your DNA is listening! With Applied Kinesiology, you will experience one of the ways your DNA talks to you. It is a way you can listen to your body's guidance in an easily understandable physical way.

Kinesiology is described as a scientific study of human movement. The term 'Applied Kinesiology' describes the practice of accessing the body's awareness of imbalances, through Manual Muscle Testing. It was discovered in 1964 by George J. Goodheart, a chiropractor, who found muscle testing could be used to obtain information from the body. He began teaching his technique to other chiropractors. Today, Applied Kinesiology has been embraced as a natural health therapy, used by not only chiropractors but naturopaths, medical doctors, dentists, nutritionists, physical therapists, massage therapists and nurse practitioners.

Based on the premise that the body has the innate ability to heal itself, muscle testing is the tool used to get feedback.

It wasn't until Dr. John F. Thie, after spending much time in the study of applied kinesiology, systemized kinesiology and began teaching lay people, that the movement took off. Believing that many of the methods of applied kinesiology could be taught and practiced as a method of self-care for all people, Dr. Thie authored the book 'Touch for Health' in 1973. Touch for Health has now become a major movement in holistic health.

Meridian Lines

According to many ancient—as well as modern—belief

systems; healthy energy flows through the meridians in a balanced way. This balance is easily disrupted through factors such as stress, emotions, poor diet and spiritual neglect. The symptoms of ill health and disease are believed to be associated with imbalances or blockages of the energy flow through these channels. With the use of applied Kinesiology, it is believed these blockages can be found and appropriate treatment discovered. Since its inception, many disciplines of kinesiology have been founded and are being practiced throughout the world.

Muscle Testing

The following is a description of the basic technique for kinesiology muscle testing as explained by John Diamond, M.D. in 'Your Body Doesn't Lie'.

Perform the following test with a friend or family member as your subject.

Have the subject stand erect, right arm relaxed at his side, left arm held out parallel to the floor with elbow straight.

Face the subject and place your left hand on his right shoulder to steady him. Then place your right hand on the subject's extended arm, just above the wrist.

Tell the subject you are going to push his arm down as he resists with all his strength.

Now push down on his arm quickly and firmly. The idea is to push just hard enough to test the spring and bounce in the arm, not so hard that the muscle becomes fatigued. It is not a question of who is stronger, but of whether the muscle can lock the shoulder joint against the push.

Was the subject able to resist the pressure? In nearly every case he will; his arm will remain extended.

Now have the subject hold something unpleasant or think of an unpleasant situation. The results will be dramatic. In nearly every case, the subject will be unable to resist the pressure. His arm will go down easily.

Self-testing is also commonly used by individuals performing applied kinesiology and can be done in various ways.

Touch your middle finger to your thumb, making a ring with each hand, linked together through each other.

Pull your right hand away from your left, but don't allow them to separate.

Repeat while focusing on an unpleasant item or thought. You should feel less resistance.

Another form of self-testing can be achieved with the use of a pendulum, while holding a weight suspended from a pivot, allowing it to swing in predetermined directions, indicating a positive or negative response.

*

*

"A wise man ought to realize that health is his most valuable possession and learn how to treat his illnesses by his own judgment."
... Hippocrates

*

There are no side effects to applied kinesiology and muscle testing. So why not give it a try and see what your body tells you? It is a technique that requires a belief and trust in one's innate abilities, which many individuals have found extremely helpful in their quest for wellbeing. Remember to have fun with this! Try it out at your next gathering. See if some people are more susceptible to this process. It's not a lie detector, but muscle testing will provide stimulating conversation. It's all about having fun in your everyday life!

*

NUMEROLOGY

If you go through the numbers representing the twelve layers of DNA, I think you will find some interesting numerological information and this will aid in your understanding of the layers. It is remarkable how all the descriptions of the layers fit so well with their numbers. Not surprisingly (but fascinating nonetheless) all the numbers in all their combinations tell the story of your DNA so well. Take some time and read the meanings of the numbers which correspond with the DNA layers. Use the formulas provided to calculate the DNA group number. I think you will find it astonishing.

The Basics of Numerology

Numerology is one of the metaphysical sciences, defined as the study of the spiritual quality of numbers and letters, recognizing that numbers have vibrations and each number vibrates differently from the next, due to the number of cycles it oscillates per second. The variation in each case is a number. Every sound, color, fragrance and thought is a vibration and each vibrates to the tune of its inherent number, each in a distinct way connected to life. In this way you can see how human life is intimately connected with numbers.

Numerology is one of the oldest sciences in history having origins in the ancient cultures of Greece, China, Rome, and Egypt while also having ties to Jewish, Christian and Islamic traditions.

This practice was revealed by Pythagoras, a sixth-century B.C. Greek mathematician and mystic who is considered the father of western numerology. Based on his perception that nature is a set of numerical relationships, divine law is defined and accurate, and that all of this can be computed through numbers, his central thought was the idea of order. All of life has a system and an order, a mathematical, musical, ethical, social and cosmic order. It was Pythagoras' view that numbers are the measurement of form and energy in the universe, which led to his system of numerology. One of the key contributions in his work was the theory that the numbers one through nine are symbolic representations of the nine stages of human life, progressing from birth through to death.

"Know thyself, then thou shalt know the universe and God."
... Pythagoras

As you explore numerology remember, as always, to have fun! If it doesn't 'feel' right to you, don't do it. Numbers only reflect the energy of the situation, using the synchronicities of the reality of your personal experience to work. Numerology is a system of numbers and numbers don't lie, but keep in mind the numbers in and of themselves, don't make things happen.

You can start with finding your personal 'set' of numbers. Your personal numbers create a template for the energy in your life; they can help you understand how to live in accordance with your own natural energy. You will learn how to calculate four of your core, or ruling, numbers, your Life Path Number, Destiny Number, Soul Number and Personality Number. These numbers can reveal a direction, a road map for achieving happiness and success in your life.

This is a very basic and ultra-simplified version of the process of numerology and can be fun to do for yourself and with friends and family. If this creates an interest please study further.

Information provided by your core numbers can be as complex as you desire, revealing more detailed information than provided here. This is a simple attempt to give you an explanation and exercises in order to form a basic understanding, which can be applied to your discussion and understanding of the Twelve Metaphysical Layers of DNA.

** Please note, when adding your numbers do NOT continue to add numbers 11, 22 and 33; they are Master Numbers and have their own meaning that will be explained below. **

Life Path Number will reveal your natural gifts and talents that will allow you to fulfill your destiny, this number is found by continually adding the numbers of the month, date and year of your birth.

To calculate your life number add together as shown, do not add individually as this will not produce the Master Numbers.

Example: August 23, 1965: 8+23+1965 = 1996, next add 1+9+9+6 = 25, next add 2+5 = 7

Destiny Number refers to your purpose and direction in life, this number is found by spelling out your birth name, finding the corresponding numbers and adding them together as shown. You may like to create a chart correlating the alphabet with numbers. A=1, B=2, C=3 and so on.

Example: Lee Jim Smith
3+5+5+1+9+4+1+4+9+2+8 = 51, next add 5+1 = 6

Soul Number exposes your heart's desire and establishes your motivation, to calculate this number add together only the vowels from your birth name as shown.

Example: Lee Jim Smith
5+5+9+9 = 28, next add 2+8 = 1

Personality Number unveils your true self and the attributes of your inner being. This number is found by adding together only the consonants of your birth name as shown.

Example Lee Jim Smith
3+1+4+1+4+2+8 = 23, next add 2+3 = 5

Now that you have your numbers what's next?

This is the fun part. Tune into your higher self! Use your innate knowing, your intuitive sense to know yourself a little better. No one knows you better than yourself, by reading the meaning to each number draw your own conclusions and you will understand yourself better.

There are no values of good or bad associated with any of the numbers. They relate to your individual journey and set of circumstances. Each number has a potential and where the numbers sit upon this scale will ultimately affect their specific meanings to you.

The commonly held definitions of each number, as used by a broad range of experienced practitioners, are as follows:

One   (1): Beginning, New, Unity, The Self

Two   (2): Connecting, Polarity, Duality

Three   (3): Creating, Inner Child

Four   (4): Building, Creation, Physical

Five   (5): Changing, Movement

Six   (6): Nurturing, Love, Sacredness

Seven   (7): Reevaluating, Divinity, Learning

Eight   (8): Expanding, Manifestation, Practical

Nine   (9): Completion, Sensitive

MASTER NUMBERS

Eleven   (11): The Spiritual Messenger

Twenty-Two   (22): The Master Builder

Thirty-Three   (33): The Master of Healing Energies through Love

*

When adding together the numbers for 'DNA Wake Up' you will not be surprised to see the following:

DNA Wake Up: 4+5+1+5+1+2+5+3+7 = 33

PERFECT!

ART, MUSIC AND DANCE

Personal creative expression of your Metaphysical DNA.

Art as a Transformative Media

Visual art has long been seen as a therapeutic tool. The introspective and profoundly personal nature of the creative arts can open an individual up to their inner feelings and beliefs.

Creating and expressing yourself artistically can be an inspiring process and a positive channel for innate communication. By tuning into your DNA through drawing, color, design and movement, new and existing energies and emotions will be discovered.

As you participate in artistic activities, listen to your inner voice and be guided from within. Focus on healing and restoring your DNA to its original state. The human body regenerates itself creating new cells constantly. We can tap in, and use this ability to let go of old patterns and create anew.

DNA Spiral

In this exercise you can create a simple way to begin your artistic dialog with your own DNA.

1- Create a simple drawing of the DNA double helix or copy the one provided.
2- Slowly fill the DNA strand with inspired colors of your JOY.
3- Fill in the space on either side with your hopes and dreams, written or drawn.

As easy as that, you have begun to communicate with your DNA.

You may repeat this exercise as often as you like, saving your art to mark your journey.

*

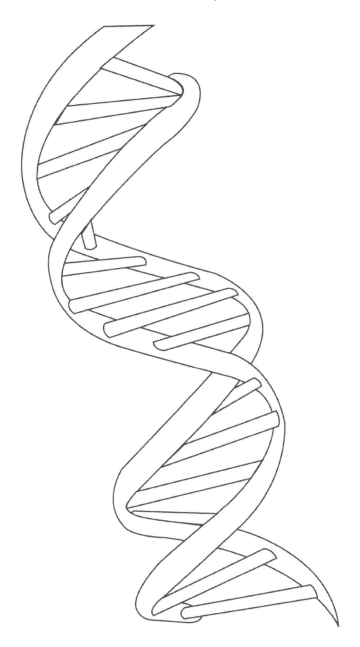

Music that Inspires

As you spend time in meditation while listening to music, you can feel the power and influence sound adds to your experience. Time spent listening to 'spiritual' music, chanting, or any sounds at all, can have an impact on your physical being and you will become aware of the effect the vibrations have on your mood.

It's a well-known fact that music affects the human body with its frequencies and vibrations. You experience the energizing effect of sound and music every time you hear a rhythmic beat. Listening to your favorite dance hit gets your toes tapping and makes you want to get your body moving.

Our health or mood can be strongly affected by music, toning, chanting, and singing.

The correct vibrational frequencies can be used to heal and balance our bodies. What does this have to do with your DNA? Tuning yourself to the proper music will aid in regenerating, renewing and waking up your DNA.

Believe what your DNA is telling you innately and listen to music that feels good. When you listen to music for reasons of growth and enlightenment open yourself up to the possibility of the vibrations moving down into your very core. The sound around that sound, that can't be heard with human ears, will find its way on a quantum level naturally to your DNA, which is being affected, moved, altered and restored to its original state.

♫ With clear intentions, miraculous things can happen with music! ♪

Free Movement and Dance

With music or without, the human body loves to move. Your DNA resides in your physical body and therefore feels all movement. You are showing appreciation and offering love to your physical body with your movement. When you combine movement with intention this offering gains power.

Dedicate time to ritual movement. Acknowledge the presence of your Metaphysical DNA and you will transport your body, with movement, to an active and alive feeling. Play with this energy by twisting and turning, expanding the organism that is your physical body. Become one with your DNA, allowing it to inspire your movements as you become an extension of all the components and layers that make up your physical being. You will feel refreshed and rejuvenated, carrying the knowledge of wellbeing within you upon completion.

Moving your physical body sends a message to your DNA that, in fact, you are aware and seeking out a positive, healthy response.

*

EPILOGUE

Together we are working towards a better world, filled with the love and light of God. It is my hope that this information will be as a spark lighting a fire within you, acting as a catalyst in your journey on Earth. This is the grandest of adventures, some of you may be stepping out of your comfort zone, and others may have felt like you were coming home. Whichever the case, what is essential to growth is conscious awareness; for once a truth has been found it will never be lost! So, you see your DNA has begun to activate you, through your intent and allowing, you hold the key to becoming a Master! With love and compassion, be easy on yourself as you step into all that you truly are.

REFERENCES

The Twelve Layers of DNA, Kryon

Genetics for Dummies, Rodden Robinson, PhD

Have a Nice DNA, Frank Balkwill and Mic Rolph

The Myth of Junk DNA, Jonathan Wells

The Complete Book of Numerology, David A. Phillips, Ph.D.

The Complete Idiot's Guide to Numerology, Second Edition

Your Body Doesn't Lie, John Diamond, MD

For further information,
Free Downloads of the Color DNA Layers
and to be kept up to date visit:
www.dnawakeup.com

Like us on Facebook:
www.facebook.com/DNAwakeup

ABOUT THE AUTHOR

Elizabeth J. Clark (Liz) received her Bachelor's Degree in Behavioral Science and Art at Westminster College of Salt Lake City in 1986. During this time she did volunteer work for Mental Health organizations and began her studies in the Sociology of Religions focusing on Native Traditions. From 1986 through 1996 Liz worked as a Psychiatric Specialist in a prominent Children's Hospital.

She has traveled to approximately sixty-two countries, researching cultural traditions. In 2003 she moved to Australia where she worked extensively with Aboriginal Youth At Risk for eight years. Liz has now returned to The United States of America where she writes privately and for DNAwakeup.com. As she continues her spiritual journey look for more works to be published in the near future.

*